GOVERNING
FOR GROWTH

Using *7 Measures of Success* to Strengthen Board Dialogue and Decision Making

BY NANCY R. AXELROD

asae & the center™
for association leadership

WASHINGTON, D.C.

The author has worked diligently to ensure that all information in this book is accurate as of the time of publication and consistent with standards of good practice in the general management community. As research and practice advance, however, standards may change. For this reason it is recommended that readers evaluate the applicability of any recommendations in light of particular situations and changing standards.

ASAE & The Center for Association Leadership
1575 I Street, NW
Washington, DC 20005-1103
Phone: (202) 626-2723; (888) 950-2723 outside the metropolitan Washington, DC
    area
Fax: (202) 220-6439
Email: books@asaecenter.org
We connect great ideas and great people to inspire leadership and achievement in the association community.

Keith C. Skillman, CAE, Vice President, Publications, ASAE & The Center for Association Leadership
Baron Williams, CAE, Director of Book Publishing, ASAE & The Center for Association Leadership

Cover design by Beth Lower, Art Director, ASAE & The Center for Association
    Leadership
Interior design by Troy Scott Parker, Cimarron Design

This book is available at a special discount when ordered in bulk quantities. For information, contact the ASAE Member Service Center at (202) 371-0940.
A complete catalog of titles is available on the ASAE & The Center for Association Leadership website at www.asaecenter.org.

ISBN-13: 978-0-88034-309-1
ISBN-10: 0-88034-309-5

Printed in the United States of America.

10 9 8 7 6 5 4 3 2 1

CONTENTS

ACKNOWLEDGEMENTS   v

Governing in Uncertain Times   1

7 Measures of Success: Abridged for Boards   5

Why the Seven Measures Matter to Boards   11

The Gap Between Theory and Practice   15

The Chief Executive Is the Linchpin for Strategic Thinking   25

Preparing Your Board for the Seven Measures   31

Closing Thoughts   39

ADDITIONAL READING AND PROGRAMS   40

ABOUT THE AUTHOR   41

ACKNOWLEDGEMENTS

THE AUTHOR AND PUBLISHER thank the ASAE & The Center for Association Leadership Research Committee for its support and the following individuals for their time, experience, and insight, which helped shape this publication. Their wisdom was invaluable.

Edward Able, Jr., President, Consulting to Associations and Nonprofits

Susan Avery, CAE, Executive Director, International Association of Plastics Distribution

Don Bretthauer, CAE, Executive Director, International Association of Administrative Professionals

Stacy Brungardt, CAE, Executive Director, Society of Teachers of Family Medicine

Hannes Combest, CAE, CEO, National Auctioneers Association

Aaron Ensminger, Manager, Communications and Publications, International Association of Administrative Professionals

Joanie Flynn, Vice President, Brand Marketing, Gaylord Hotels

Paul Greeley, Jr., President, Signature Group, Inc.

Nancy Green, CAE, Executive Director, National Association for Gifted Children

John Healy, CAE, CEO, National Association of Insurance and Financial Advisors

Jill Kliethermes, CEO, Missouri Nurses Association

Carolyn Lanham, Senior Director, Executive Operations, American Institute of Architects

John Mamone, CAE, Chief Financial Officer, The Alliance to Save Energy

Toni Samuel, CAE, Executive Director, American Society for Public Administration

Jody Shelton, Executive Director, American Association of School Personnel Administrators

Tiffany Shepherd, CAE, Deputy Director, American Institute of Architects Kansas City

Roger Sherwood, CAE, retired from Society of Teachers of Family Medicine

Karen Tucker Thomas, CAE, President/Founder, KST Consulting, LLC

Cathlene Williams, CAE, Cathlene Williams, LLC

7 Measures programs are sponsored by **Gaylord Hotels,** an ASAE & The Center Strategic Partner committed to making associations become more remarkable.

GAYLORD HOTELS®
A Gaylord Entertainment Company

Governing in
Uncertain Times

THE ROLE OF GOVERNING boards has never been more
important. Economic turbulence, growing scrutiny from
regulators, and greater competition from other nonprofit
and for-profit entities are pressuring associations and other
similar organizations to become more effective in delivering value.
Associations that do not invest in the strategies that build short- and
long-term organizational sustainability are likely to lose muscle and
competitive edge, if not members. Battening down the hatches and
riding out the storm will probably not be the best strategy to make
organizations better and stronger during these challenging times.

The best leaders must navigate two fronts. First, they must govern
and manage to meet today's challenges. Second, they should be
positioned to adapt in order to thrive in tomorrow's world. An
unintended consequence of focusing on immediate problems will
be neglect of long-term opportunities. These challenging times call
for a culture of inclusion, adaptability, innovation, sustainability,
and resilience that inspires members, staff, and volunteers. Boards
that are either disengaged or enmeshed in the thicket of operations

deprive their organizations of their collective intelligence to help attain and sustain high performance.

∾

"Preserve the Core/Stimulate Progress.
*Enduring great organizations are characterized by
a fundamental duality. On the one hand, they have
a set of timeless core values and a core reason for
being that remain constant over long periods of time.
On the other hand, they have a relentless drive for
change and progress, a creative compulsion that often
manifests in BHAGs (Big Hairy Audacious Goals).
Great organizations keep clear the difference between
their core values, which never change, and operating
strategies and cultural practices, which endlessly adapt
to a changing world."*
**—7 Measures of Success: What Remarkable
Associations Do That Others Don't**

In 2006, ASAE & The Center for Association Leadership published *7 Measures of Success: What Remarkable Associations Do That Others Don't*. (The complete book is available at www.asaecenter.org/bookstore.) The research for the book adapted the matched-pair methodology used by Jim Collins to develop his seminal work *Good to Great,* and in fact, Collins advised the "Measures of Success" researchers, who scoured 15 years of data to address this question: What distinguishes a remarkable association from a merely good one?

The study, as the book title suggests, identified seven key factors found in associations that remain remarkable year after year. At a glance, any of the seven measures may seem largely what- and how-focused—and hence predominately the domain of association staff charged with executing. Look a bit deeper, though, and it is abundantly clear that each of the seven measures has *policy and strategy* implications that fall squarely in the purview of any board of directors that aspires to play a strategic role. Boards of directors, in particular, must concern themselves with purpose, strategy, and accountability—which comprise a thread that runs through *7 Measures of Success.*

With the help of a follow-up *7 Measures of Success Implementation Guide & Assessment Tool,* a growing number of association leaders are integrating or drawing from the *7 Measures* framework as an assessment and planning tool for the staff. Since *7 Measures* explores important issues that should be pondered in the boardroom, association executives are asking how to engage their boards in the process. *This publication has been written to help chief executives, board members, and senior staff professionals use the seven measures as a practical tool for enlisting the board's collective horsepower to strengthen an organization's capacity to perform and adapt.*

This guide provides an overview of the opportunities and challenges in enlisting your board in the seven measures as a tool to advance the board's strategic role. A complementary *Facilitator's Guide* provides resources for designing, customizing, and implementing strategic thinking discussions for each specific measure.

7 Measures of Success: Abridged for Boards

W HAT FOLLOWS IS A summary of the seven traits identified through the ASAE & The Center study. The intent of this synopsis is to provide board members in particular with a baseline for strategic dialogue about organizational performance and continual improvement. In fact, whether or not your association is "implementing" the seven measures, per se, the themes themselves are likely to emerge in important discussions in association offices and boardrooms. The seven measures can provide a robust framework for strategic thinking and informed decision making by board members.

Measure 1: A Customer Service Culture

In remarkable associations, the needs and challenges faced by members always take precedence. Remarkable associations build their structures, processes, and interactions—their entire culture—around assessing and fulfilling members' needs and expectations. This unity of purpose permeates the entire organization. Everyone—staff, leaders, and members alike—knows who the

ASK THESE SEVEN QUESTIONS

Typically, staff members are delegated the primary responsibility of implementing policies pertaining to each of the seven measures of success. Under some circumstances—for instance, because an organization has a very small staff or because the nature of the measure of success demands it—individual board members may take a more direct role in implementation. However, for each of the seven measures, the board's primary role should be asking and addressing big-picture questions such as the following seven:

- What do we do well in fulfilling this measure? For example, to what degree do we have a customer-service culture?
- What could we do better?
- What are the emerging new trends, best practices, or new opportunities we should consider that could enhance our capacity?
- What metrics will best measure progress in strengthening our performance in this area?
- What resources might be needed to improve our capacity to deliver against this measure of success?
- What impediments are most likely to hamper our progress against this measure?
- How can the board add the greatest value in enhancing our organization's ability in this area?

association serves and keeps the member not only at center stage but in the spotlight. No one presumes to decide what the member needs without asking first and then listening to the answer.

Measure 2:
Alignment of Products and Services With Mission

Continually successful associations consistently find ways to connect their reason for being to their programs and services. While offerings vary, what never changes is the consistent focus on linking those offerings to mission. That focus rarely wavers, even as external forces, societal changes, and developments within a membership occur. New initiatives and changes to existing programs and services flow from one central question: What do our constituents need *today* to achieve the mission we have always had? Remarkable associations view members as a population to serve rather than as a market to sell to. In fact, they reject out-of-hand a product or service that fails to directly aid their members, even if it might generate revenue.

Measure 3: Data-Driven Strategies

Remarkable associations continually track member needs and issues as well as the wider environment; then they collectively analyze the data to reach a shared understanding through asking, "What do we now know? What are we going to do about it?" These associations then incorporate the findings into their strategic and operational planning. But the data collection doesn't stop there. It continues through another methodical, disciplined cycle of gathering, analyzing, and making changes because of what was learned. Remarkable associations also face the facts: They do not presume that they know better than what the data tell them. When new data demonstrate that the present course, no matter how well conceived, is in error, remarkable associations do not hesitate to make adjustments.

Measure 4: Dialogue and Engagement

Although remarkable associations have developed an expertise in gathering information, they know that is not enough. They also nurture a culture in which the information is analyzed and shared throughout the organization. Everyone, not only senior managers and elected leaders, is expected to use that data to figure out what actions the data are demanding of the organization. Characteristic of these organizations is a close-knit, consistent culture in which all employees not only receive the same script, in the form of the same information, but also see the potential to contribute to a blockbuster production. Whether they have lead or supporting roles or work behind the scenes is not relevant. Rather, they all share equally in the responsibility to contribute and add value to the association. Remarkable associations reflect a neighborhood culture characterized by shared values and a unified purpose.

Measure 5: CEO as a Broker of Ideas

The CEO is the great go-between—the individual who must not only understand the organization's vision but also be able to engage others in defining, refining, and responding to that vision and all it entails. While the CEO may be a visionary, what's more important is that the he or she has the ability to facilitate visionary thinking throughout the organization. What matters is not the CEO's vision but the members' vision. The CEO plays a key role in creating a vision for the organization. That role, however, rests with gathering consensus around a member-generated vision rather than forcing buy-in to a personal vision. In remarkable associations, the CEO helps both elected leaders and staff members think in terms of what is possible and enables things to happen rather than decreeing it so.

Measure 6: Organizational Adaptability

Less-than-remarkable organizations tend to react more slowly to crises or setbacks than do remarkable associations. As revealed in the study, a frequent response of "comparison organizations" was to continue what they were already doing but more intensely, hoping that the extra effort would resolve the crisis or setback. In contrast, remarkable associations not only weather crises—assessing and taking action quickly—but they learn from them and, where warranted, make course changes with a long view in mind. Whether or not a change is anticipated, remarkable organizations maintain a clear understanding of their core purpose and willingly adapt how they do business to remain consistent with that purpose.

Measure 7: Alliance Building

Forming effective alliances is high on the priority list of many associations. The factor that distinguishes remarkable associations is their approach to alliances. Remarkable associations pursue alliances that relate to existing strategies or that form a tight fit with their mission and purpose. In that regard, they determine with whom *not* to partner as much as with whom they should partner. Secure in their identity and what they bring to the table, these associations communicate clear expectations for each specific partnership. They're willing to admit that they cannot do everything on their own. But they do not hesitate to walk away if a win-win situation does not materialize. As in their approach to each of the measures of success, remarkable associations do not stray from clearly stated goals, and they maintain a disciplined process to achieve those goals.

Why the Seven Measures Matter to Boards

ONE OF THE CONVENTIONAL ways for a board to help set the association's direction and priorities is to participate in the formulation of a strategic plan. But without the capacity to either execute the plan or adjust course as needed, a strategic plan is merely a set of magnificent intentions. While boards have become more engaged in the strategic planning process, they often lack the means to monitor organizational performance or to assess whether there is adequate infrastructure to support the organization's priorities.

Regardless of how engaged the board has been in creating the strategic plan, the presence of this document does not demonstrate the board's capacity for ongoing strategic thinking. Most organizations move though stages of development as well as cycles of progress and decline. It is difficult to be at the top of the high-performing curve over long periods of time. It is difficult to reach high-performing status at all when the board is not awake to critical environmental changes or operational strategies that will drive performance improvement. How well the board and the executive management team deal with emerging issues, unexpected opportunities, and ambiguous threats may well determine the organization's success, if not its very survival.

"Strategic planning has not only never amounted to strategic thinking, but has, in fact, often impeded it."
—Henry Mintzberg

Most boards receive plenty of information. Unfortunately, it is not always tailored to the governance responsibilities of the board. Everything that can be measured does not necessarily count, and everything that counts cannot always be measured. If the management team does not provide the board with the right metrics and reporting practices, boards may not be monitoring the right stuff, as illustrated in the two examples in the sidebar below.

At many organizations, it is apparent that the board is more attentive to strategic planning than strategic thinking. When the organization's strategic imperatives do not find their way into the board's work, the board is less capable of separating the whales

---

GOVERNANCE-ORIENTED INFORMATION

The board of an association foundation that wants to increase its revenue from individual donations does not learn how well it is succeeding by looking exclusively at the resources the foundation invests in this effort. The board should be receiving and tracking outcomes such as the number and amount of donations, the types of individuals who donate, and the fundraising activities that seem to yield the best return on investment. Similarly, if an association has a strategic objective to expand its strategic alliances, the number of new relationships will be less informative to the board than how well the staff provides the board with outputs such as the number of high-quality relationships with targeted organizations that provide mutual benefit and increased influence to advance mission.

from the paramecia. The seven measures provide a framework to help boards understand, monitor, and respond to key questions regarding institutional performance that will inform board dialogue and decision making in real time.

The board has overall fiduciary responsibility for the organization and the products and services it provides. Board members of both investor-owned and nonprofit corporations are expected to serve as stewards to protect the assets of the organization. This fiduciary role requires governing boards to make many decisions that shape the organization's direction and performance. The most effective boards ask themselves what kind of information they and the staff need in order for the organization to succeed. They ensure that the staff has the support to gather that information and to use it in their work. And they recognize the board's own critical role in building and sustaining organizational capacity. Continuous evaluation and improvement form the key pathway to high performance. Strategic dialogues on the seven measures can equip the board to carry out its oversight, stewardship, and strategic thinking responsibilities.

Exploring the Seven Measures Helps Boards Go to the Balcony

Two of the most important concepts in a leader's toolkit are context and perspective. But it is easy for association leaders to get caught up in responding to the problems of the day and to under-invest in viewing the big picture to be responsive to opportunities and threats. One of the qualities ascribed to star athletes is their capacity to play hard while keeping the whole game enterprise in mind as if they stood on a balcony above the field of play. Like stellar athletes, the best boards try not to get swept up in the daily fray of tactics and immediate problems. Rather, they scan the horizon and calibrate the association's appropriate pace of change for the industry or profession they serve.

"You should only change as fast as you need to, but that is still faster than most organizations are capable of today."
—Gary Hamel, Associations Now, April 2009

Strategic thinking discussions of the seven measures can help boards have thoughtful conversations with their staffs about how well both volunteers and staff professionals cultivate the strongest predictors of great performance. The *7 Measures of Success* findings can't give you the easy-to-read roadmap to success, because the benchmarks of remarkable associations require disciplined thought and disciplined actions. The seven measures that distinguish remarkable nonprofit organizations from their less remarkable counterparts *can* provide a strategic framework to help boards periodically go to the balcony to explore the big issues and best practices that exert the greatest impact on institutional performance.

It would be unfair to suggest that these seven measures are ignored by boards. While many boards and board committees address these issues, two things are often missing from their deliberations. The first is contextual information at the governance level that enables board members to assess emerging risks, explore best practices, and discern opportunities for growth. The second is practical tools to generate options for adaptive change for continuous improvement. What boards are not always invited to do is to make a discernible difference in influencing strategic outcomes. As indicated in the board-related questions in the preceding section on the abridged version of *7 Measures of Success,* all seven measures have governance implications that can benefit from the board's active role in understanding and responding to the critical trends, ideas, challenges, and strategies embedded in each measure.

The Gap Between Theory and Practice

BOARDS THAT GOVERN AND staff members who manage
associations operate in a climate that demands greater
accountability for ethical and legal conduct. Inadequate
board performance has contributed substantially to poor organizational performance. Well-publicized financial and behavior scandals
at nonprofit as well as for-profit organizations have lowered public
trust and heightened scrutiny from legislators, regulators, the
press, and members. While there is little evidence of corruption or
malfeasance at the board level, one of the common culprits appears
to be "non-governance." When it comes to the board, what has
been missing in action is a governance culture of accountability,
diligence, and inquiry.

Financial turmoil, unprecedented innovation in information
technology and systems, impending generational change, and
powerful forces in the professions and industries associations
serve have created new expectations of how boards should
operate. Boards that are passive, complacent, or inclined to
accept questionable performance are abdicating their stewardship

responsibility as well as their potential to add even greater value. In short, boards are now expected to focus on critical issues, measure success, and be actively engaged in envisioning future directions and shaping strategy.

Nonprofit organizations must navigate the faster and deeper pace of internal and external change by harnessing the intellectual and social capital of their boards during these turbulent times. Their boards must be capable of not only understanding key drivers of change but also of monitoring their impact and adjusting course when necessary. While the scope and pace of change may be quickening, what has not changed is the clarion call for boards to play a strategic role as leaders as well as a fiduciary role as stewards. This recurring lament from association leaders suggests that there is more to good governance than compliance. *In addition to oversight, boards need to provide insight and, if possible, foresight.*

"The greatest danger in times of turbulence is not the turbulence. It is to act with yesterday's logic."
—Peter Drucker

A Question of Value

There is no simple formula to cultivate strategic thinking from the board. Boards that play a predominantly strategic role do not simply evolve. They are constructed and enabled by an intentional, systematic, and ongoing effort by board and staff members to focus the board's attention on what matters most to the organization's future performance and viability. Perhaps most important of all, they are empowered by clarity and consensus from board and staff on the answers to two fundamental questions: "What kind of a board do we want?" and "What are the best mechanisms to engage the full range of abilities and expertise that will be needed from our board members?"

Association leaders are not always candid about the level of engagement they welcome from their boards. The common lament from board and staff members for their board members to be more strategic is tantamount to baying at the moon in an organization in which the board is not viewed as a genuine strategic asset that needs support to operate at the highest and best use of its collective capacity. Best practices and governance tools are toothless when either chief executives or chief elected officers view their boards as merely legal necessities, compliance mechanisms, or headaches to be endured.

The highest-performing boards do not manage programs or implement their own polices when competent staff are in place. Boards can add the greatest value when they focus on the strategic and policy matters that ultimately will determine their organizations' success. But this does not require them to become bobble heads who abdicate their fiduciary responsibilities for oversight and decision making.

The incessant, rhythmic thump of the rubber stamp in the boardroom can be mitigated by constructive skepticism, healthy debate, and good and timely questions from board members. There will be times when red flags related to changes in performance indicators, potential mismanagement or ethical violations, or changes in regulatory requirements may well require more active board engagement in management to avoid the board culture of passivity and acquiescence in organizations that have become poster children for governance breakdowns. It may not always be clear whether a board is guilty of meddlesome interference or responsible oversight until after the fact, with the wisdom of hindsight.

"In many organizations, the board is viewed in a way similar to an appendix, a part of the body without apparent purpose but capable of serious inconvenience. The combination of apparent superfluity with the capacity to inflict real discomfort makes many question the need to have a board. Seeing only their inconvenience and failing to understand their value are strong disincentives to invest in their competence and effectiveness."

—***Nonprofit Boards That Work,*** **by Maureen Robinson, published by John Wiley and Sons**

Recognizing and Surmounting Barriers to Strategic Governance

Steering an association through times of change is a leadership responsibility. It becomes a more perilous journey if the multiple and diverse assets that boards and board members bring to their organizations are not fully leveraged. But to be effective, boards need to focus on those issues and priorities vital to enhancing the organization's future.

Boards should not be intervening directly in operations or micromanaging every transaction that management negotiates. High-performing, high-impact boards focus more on forward-looking issues than threshing through the weeds of *administrivia*. So why is this not the prevailing practice? Why are boards often criticized as under-involved, inappropriately engaged, or unclear about their responsibilities? Why do association leaders often complain that their boards tend to operate more like assemblies of managers rather than to govern as leaders?

∾

"Why does there generally seem to be an inverse correlation between the importance of a matter and the time accorded to it in our board meetings?"
—A frustrated board chair

Democracy is the worst form of government, Winston Churchill said, except for all the other ones. The same might be said of nonprofit boards. Unfortunately, many boards are not as strong as they can or should be. While most boards aspire to play a strategic role, the dirty little secret is that they often lack the capacity to function effectively in this domain. To overcome the inherent tendency of board members to gravitate to short-term, tactical matters, it is important to understand why strategic thinking is not a natural act for most boards. To make strategic thinking a part of regular, ongoing board work, board officers and the staff members who support them must comprehend and overcome the following eight barriers:

- In their day jobs, individual board members typically serve as practitioners. As professionals, they are often expected to manage rather than to govern. Likened to members of a symphony orchestra, many board members are rewarded in their non-volunteer work for their performance as composers, conductors, or soloists. Even if they perform in jobs that are comparable to team musicians, they do not bring years of training to their governance performances, rarely study for their role within a board, and have limited practice time as board members.

• Nonprofit board members often lack experience serving on groups comparable to governing boards, in which each member shares equal power and makes decisions requiring consensus. When board members do bring experience on other boards, it is often from the boards of affiliates or smaller organizations that are primarily volunteer-driven. The latter often require board members to function both as board members and part-time administrators to compensate for a small staff or no staff.

"The role of the members of the national association board is very different from that of a board member of an affiliate. Frequently, as an affiliate board member you wear many hats, including administrative responsibilities to help support a small or non-existent staff. Affiliate boards also tend to do much of their work as a committee of the whole. I don't think I had a clear picture of my role as a national director when I first came on the board."
—Comment from a seasoned board member during a board orientation program of a large professional society

• Too many organizations wait until the board-orientation process to explain the role of the board and the responsibilities and expectations of its individual members. Without an adequate job description available to nominating committees and board candidates, the learning curve to help new board members contribute to the collective and strategic work of the board is considerably steeper.

- While an increasing number of nonprofit organizations has recognized the need for and invested in building internal capacity to strengthen organizational effectiveness, the need to cultivate the leadership capacity of the board is sometimes overlooked. Making strategic thinking a group norm takes time, effort, and discipline. If staff or board leaders neglect this investment in board development, it will not occur by osmosis.

- Paradoxically, staff members can inadvertently invite the board to micromanage by providing predominately *administrative* information to board members. Board members will respond in kind to the level of the information that is shared with them. And too much of that information tends to be administratively rather than governance oriented. The absence of meaningful information that empowers the board to monitor progress from a strategic vantage point does not just mitigate the board's fiduciary oversight. It tends to encourage board members to either meddle in the operational or base more of their actions on opinions rather than on information and knowledge.

  For example, board members can't provide financial oversight if they don't know what to look for. Providing the board a detailed budget with every line item will invite board members to question even the most minor items that interest them. Financial information presented to the board should focus on fiduciary oversight questions such as whether the financial plan is consistent with the strategic plan, if cash flow is projected to be adequate, or whether the board has ensured that internal controls over expenditures are in place.

- Board committees and task forces often replicate the organizational chart. When board work teams mirror and monitor staff functions, it is difficult for individual board members *not* to function as either surrogate administrators or staff supervisors in fulfilling their roles. Board standing committees and task forces should reflect the association's and the board's strategic priorities, not the organization's administrative structure, its traditions, or the personal interests of individual board members.

• Individual board members have responsibilities but not personal authority to make organizational decisions. While the collective board is expected to govern and make decisions, individual board members are typically asked to execute operational tasks to support the work of the board and the organization (e.g., leadership of task forces, speaking engagements, fundraising, member recruitment, and other assignments). Board members

---

◆ ◆ ◆ ◆ ◆ ◆ ◆

PUTTING ORGANIZATIONAL INTERESTS ABOVE INDIVIDUAL INTERESTS

The challenge of learning to put the interests of the organization before one's personal or professional interests is illuminated in the following observations from new board chairs who have attended ASAE and the Center's Exceptional Boards program during the past few years.

• "It is difficult for board members not to allow their votes to be unduly influenced by loyalty to their denominations."

• "After the board votes on a controversial issue, disgruntled association members will often contact individual board members to complain to find out how board members voted. I try to help new board members understand that the best response we can give them is to explain how the board tried to do what was best for the organization in arriving at this decision."

• "I learned that one of the hardest parts of becoming the chair is to become the spokesperson for important positions the board takes that do not necessarily reflect my personal or professional views."

who are expected to both govern collectively and to support the organization individually can easily confuse their roles by trying to either implement in the boardroom or govern in their volunteer leadership assignments.

- The high turnover rate in association boards makes strategic work more elusive. In the association world, both the chief elected officer and approximately one third of the board typically change every year. New board members do not bring the same level of engagement in either developing the strategic priorities or honoring the governance practices that have evolved. This makes it more difficult to sustain the kind of board leadership continuity that can strengthen boards whose members have more time serving together and practicing how to work collectively as a group. Annual changes in board composition and leadership require an ongoing investment in board development and continuing education to both sustain what works and improve the board's structure, practices, and performance.

"Frequently new board members come to the board orientation with all kinds of new ideas that they feel are their 'pet projects' for their tenure on the board. New board members are wonderful sources for new ideas, but they have to be willing to put aside any preconceived ideas about what they want to do as a director. There is always room for new ideas, but there is an appropriate time for them to be introduced."
—A board president of a trade association

The Chief Executive Is the Linchpin for Strategic Thinking

A BOARD'S ABILITY TO EXERCISE wise oversight and contribute meaningful insight rests in part on the information executives give them and the way in which they help boards allocate their time. One of the things that distinguishes remarkable associations from the comparison group in *7 Measures of Success* is that the CEO plays a key role in vision—not by imposing his or her personal vision but by *facilitating visionary thinking throughout the organization*. This is consistent with other leadership studies that highlight the chief executive officer's capacity to simultaneously lead *and* empower. "The CEO as a broker of ideas," the fifth measure of success, is essential to an association's success in engaging the board effectively in the seven measures.

The *7 Measures* research found that in remarkable associations, the CEO

- Operates as a broker of ideas.
- Engages others in defining, refining, and responding to the organization's vision.

- Elicits and inspires the thinking of others in a shared vision for the organization.
- Listens and is open to others' ideas.
- Stimulates energy and fosters effective communication, engagement, and collaborative action among and between staff and volunteers.
- Is willing to step aside at times to facilitate a discussion of ideas without dictating an outcome.
- Helps both elected leaders and staff think in terms of what is possible.
- Enables things to happen rather than decreeing what will happen.

Team of Rivals: The Political Genius of Abraham Lincoln, *Doris Kearns Goodwin's biography of Abraham Lincoln, provides lessons for the chief executive officer and board leaders about the tone at the top. Lincoln's capacity to surround himself with smart people (many of whom were rivals, disgruntled opponents, and strong egos) who felt free to argue with him and challenge his assumptions informed and improved his decisions.*

The board's ability to respond to the challenges it confronts will depend on how well informed the CEO helps it become about the organization it governs. Providing the board with the right information in accordance with its governance responsibilities while taking care not to duplicate administration's responsibilities will help the board think and act strategically. Over time, the chief executive officer contributes (along with others) to the pattern of beliefs, traditions, and practices that define the board's governance culture and engagement level. A CEO who serves as "the great go between" is in a better position to provide the board with the right tools to conduct the strategic thinking discussions of the seven

A CULTURE OF INQUIRY

When board members are not encouraged to seek information from multiple sources, question assumptions, and engage in constructive deliberation, it is much easier for the group to resort to group think, to reject multiple sources of information, or to defer to the dominant voices. Boards that foster a culture of inquiry are in the best position to engage in a strategic thinking discussion of the seven measures. The norms that characterize a culture of inquiry include

- A sense of mutual respect, trust, and inclusiveness among board members
- The capacity to explore divergent views in a respectful rather than adversarial manner
- A willingness to gather information to inform decisions
- Equal access to information
- The presence of active feedback mechanisms that help the board engage in continuous improvement
- An individual and collective commitment to decisions, plans of action, and accountability to follow through on the board's agreements

Source: *Culture of Inquiry: Healthy Debate in the Boardroom,* by Nancy R. Axelrod, published by BoardSource

measures described in this publication as well as the companion *Facilitator's Guide.*

While many CEOs may not quite have perfected the heroic, ideal broker role as defined in *7 Measures of Success,* every CEO must be willing to engage the board as an ally in pursuit of organizational excellence to implement a successful strategic thinking discussion. The board, in turn, is responsible for both holding the chief executive accountable and providing support that enables him or her to be successful. A committed, informed, and proactive board that works collaboratively with the CEO is better positioned to use the seven measures as a vehicle to sharpen dialogue and decision making.

$$\backsim$$

"At the end of each board meeting we typically ask ourselves if we were too operational or strategic enough."
—A board chair who attended ASAE & The Center's Exceptional Boards Program

Adapting and applying the seven measures framework and the other ideas offered in this publication will require staff and board time. The chief executive and the management team, as well as board leadership, must invest time in preparing a board to act strategically, regardless of the issue that warrants the board's attention. Once there is consensus on the board's preeminent role and its key responsibilities, practices that organizations use to empower their boards to act in a more strategic manner include the following:

- Nomination and election of board members based on written competencies, qualifications, and other criteria
- Orientation programs that acquaint new board members with board member responsibilities and expectations as well as the organization's history and culture
- Continuing education programs that keep the board abreast of trends and issues in the profession or industry, good governance, and society
- Strategic plans with measurable goals and critical indicators to monitor performance
- A job description that defines the role of the board as a collective group as well as the responsibilities and expectations of its individual members

- An annual board work plan
- Joint board-staff efforts to frame and explore issues
- Board meeting agendas that allocate sufficient time for discussion of important issues to enable the board to deliberate before action is required at a subsequent meeting
- Board agendas and priorities aligned with strategic planning goals and agendas
- Reinforcement of the board's attention to priorities by providing key questions for discussion in advance of meetings
- Time at each meeting for the chief executive to discuss future issues
- Use of a consent agenda
- Monitoring of the use of board time and attention
- Labeling of board agenda items to help board members understand how each item is related to the board's or the organization's strategic priorities and what deliverable the board is being asked to provide (e.g., communication to the board, or consultation or action requested from the board)
- Periodic assessment of the performance of the board, individual board members, and board committees to improve board performance and effectiveness
- A constructive and humane process for annual performance assessment of the chief executive
- Development of a board information system that
    - Helps the board understand the big picture
    - Helps the board discharge its specific responsibilities
    - Presents information in a clear and concise manner to make the most of the board's limited time to analyze information

- Provides context (i.e. current information is compared with projections, trends, or comparison groups, with variances highlighted)
- Is both accurate and credible to be responsive to the ultimate accountability of the board

Preparing Your Board for the Seven Measures

H IGH-ACHIEVING BOARDS, AND THEIR committees, are able to think and act strategically. Using the seven measures to allot a time and a discipline to strategic thinking is one way to help your board contribute to your organization's success. But each organization must determine when as well as how to use the seven measures as a governance tool. For example, some organizations might engage the board in a comprehensive process of reviewing all of the measures prior to launching a strategic planning process or an executive leadership transition. Others will select one measure for the board to address when it is time to revisit, adjust, or overhaul policies and practices embedded in that measure. Others will select a measure that reflects low-hanging fruit because the measure is the one most amenable to improvement.

This guide is designed to help board and staff leaders engage their boards in tackling matters of strategic magnitude. For the board to work with the seven measures, it is helpful but not essential for it to have experience operating in the strategic realm. A board that plays

◆ ◆ ◆ ◆ ◆ ◆ ◆

PERIODIC BOARD ASSESSMENTS

One of the major strengths of a periodic assessment of the board and its members is that it allots a specific time, a priority, and a forum to the board's self-improvement. Board self-assessment approaches range from the informal to the formal. Mechanisms for board evaluation include

- Board meeting evaluations
- Discussion of critical incidents that provide teachable moments for the board to learn from its breakdowns or breakthroughs
- Exit interviews with board members at the end of their terms
- Mini board self-assessment questionnaires that invite board members to provide a snapshot of the board's effectiveness
- Formal board self-assessment diagnostic tools that invite board members to assess the collective performance of the board as well as their individual contributions

a predominantly strategic role is more likely to have processes and structures in place to gather relevant information, define the right questions underlying important issues, explore divergent views, and challenge assumptions in order to inform decisions. Regardless of the current level of engagement of your board, designing and implementing strategic discussions based on the seven measures can provide your board with valuable practice time for the ongoing process of thinking and acting strategically that should characterize a significant portion of its work.

While *7 Measures of Success* can enhance your board's and your association's performance, there is no one-size-fits-all way to integrate the measures into the board's deliberations. A board's governance culture can be passive or assertive, complacent or diligent. A board might be eager to ratify management's recommendations or more inclined to challenge assumptions. Like the choice

WHY DO THE SEVEN MEASURES HAVE CONSEQUENCES FOR POLICY AND STRATEGY THAT MERIT THE BOARD'S TIME AND ATTENTION?

- They influence the organization's effectiveness in building organizational capacity.

- They are predictors of organizational performance and adaptability.

- They have consequences for how the organization will continue to do business in light of changing trends.

- They are core to the mission.

- They influence the way in which the organization practices accountability and transparency.

- They are likely to require board action if significant policy or program changes are required.

- The chief executive may require the board's support to ensure that sufficient resources are allocated to sustain or grow related programs or practices.

of governance policies and practices, the application of the seven measures should be based on the size and scope of your organization, its culture, and its unique circumstances. It should also be based on the objectives and outcomes you expect from your board. Readers are encouraged to adapt rather than merely adopt the ideas in this publication.

Board Forums and Formats for Advancing Strategic Discussions

Most associations are better at executing their current program of work than they are at adapting to improve organizational capacity in light of critical changes in the profession or industry they serve. Boards often tackle problems without exploring the context, seeking

FRAMING AND SUMMARIZING
ISSUES FOR STRATEGIC DISCUSSION

To advance strategic thinking from the board, leaders, and staff of The National Court Reporters Association frame issues on which their board must deliberate or take action in the following format prior to board meetings.

NCRA Format for Issues Papers to Be Presented to the Board

Issue:	A single sentence or title that identifies the topic to be addressed.
Background:	A brief paragraph or two describes how the issue emerged, summarizes any past history that would be useful in creating a context for considering the issue, and provides current status.
Discussion:	Outlines and briefly discusses the various options available, ramifications of action (or inaction), pros and cons, and other general analysis of the issue.
Objective(s):	Explicitly states the action being requested from the board. Examples include: 1. Formal board action, in which case a draft motion is presented 2. More general direction from the board on desired next steps for the committee/staff 3. Indication that this is an item to be addressed as a strategic dialogue
Attachments:	Any relevant back-up material (correspondence, data, reports, etc.) that might assist the board in making an informed decision should be listed here and attached following this issue paper.

Source: Reprinted by permission of the National Court Reporters Association

continued on next page

NCRA Summary of Board Strategic Dialogue

This report summarizes the ideas generated by the board outside of a formal, business session. Unless subsequently addressed by formal action of the board, it does not necessarily represent consensus of the board nor should the presence of an item in this report be construed as commitment to accept or implement the recommended action.

TITLE
Date
City, State

Issue Statement:

Discussion Points:

Options Considered:

help from experts, or identifying the right questions and issues before options are considered. Rather than giving the answers, *7 Measures* can help the board think about the right questions. Once the right questions are framed, it becomes easier for the board to identify obstacles and opportunities, revisit assumptions, generate options, and probe feasibility *before* moving to a decision or action.

"The significant problems we face cannot be solved at the same level of thinking we were at when we created them."
—Albert Einstein

The potential outcomes of using a tool like *7 Measures* for continuous learning include greater productivity, more meaningful engagement, and improved performance for the board, the staff, and the organization. While the board's effectiveness and performance can be enhanced by the dialogue and constructive debate that the seven measures should invite from boards, unfortunately board retreats and strategic thinking forums are sometimes viewed as unwanted distractions that interfere with the comfort of "business as usual." A key to the success of customizing the seven measures for board work is getting the buy-in and engagement from the participants at the front end of the process.

To determine when and which measure or measures is most important for the board to address, a good first step is to ask the board and the management team to identify the critical issues that warrant the greatest time and attention over the next year. In preparation for the strategic thinking discussion of the seven measures, consider inviting board and staff members to complete a brief electronic survey that includes questions such as the following:

- How would you rank our effectiveness in executing each of the seven measures on a scale of 1–5 (one being least effective and 5 being most effective)?
- Which one of the seven measures could the association address for quickest success?
- Which measure will take the longest to implement?
- Which measure warrants the greatest engagement from our board and staff during the next 6–12 months?

Board members often complain about the scripted and mind-numbing nature of their meetings. When board members are given either too much information with too little perspective or limited opportunities to influence strategic outcomes, there is a greater chance that they will either tune out or act out in inappropriate ways. To circumvent this danger, it is becoming more common for board meeting agendas to include a "strategic" issue that does not necessarily require a vote but does require the board's critical thinking and input. (As one example, the tool developed by the National Court Reporters Association to help the board effectively engage and act is included in this chapter.)

Each of the seven measures is a good candidate for this agenda item. This can be done either by allotting time within a board meeting agenda or by focusing an entire board meeting on a single overarching topic such as customer service or alliance building that demands the board's time and attention.

Closing Thoughts

"The dogmas of the quiet past are inadequate to the stormy present... As our case is new, we must think and act anew."
—Abraham Lincoln

ELL PUBLICIZED CASES OF mismanagement, malfeasance, or non-governance have pushed the work of boards to the top of the public and professional agenda. While new regulations and more active self-regulation will help promote accountability and transparency, they will not help boards understand their businesses better, drive strategic direction, or evaluate new opportunities and risks. When adapted to fit an association board's needs, the seven measures can encourage strategic thinking to leverage your board's role as a strategic asset. The companion *Facilitator's Guide* to this publication includes case studies, resources, and suggestions on embedding and customizing strategic dialogues in board meetings to help boards allocate time to what matters most.

ADDITIONAL READING AND PROGRAMS

- *7 Measures of Success: What Remarkable Associations Do That Others Don't,* 2006 ASAE & The Center for Association Leadership.

- *7 Measures of Success Implementation Guide & Assessment Tool,* 2008 ASAE & The Center for Association Leadership.

- Companion *Governing for Growth Facilitator's Guide,* 2009 ASAE & The Center for Association Leadership.

- *Supporting The Decision to Join: What Association Boards Should Know and Do About Membership and Affiliation,* by James Dalton, 2009 ASAE & The Center for Association Leadership.

- *The Volunteer Leadership Issue of Associations Now,* published annually by ASAE & The Center for Association Leadership.

- *The Source: Twelve Principles of Governance That Power Exceptional Boards,* 2005 BoardSource.

- *Culture of Inquiry: Healthy Debate in the Boardroom,* by Nancy R. Axelrod, 2007 BoardSource.

- In addition to other programs, ASAE & The Center for Association Leadership offer two programs dedicated to helping teams of chief executive officers and chief elected officers enhance the board's performance. Visit www.asaecenter.org/programsevents for the latest calendar and list of programs.

ABOUT THE AUTHOR

Nancy R. Axelrod is a governance consultant who provides services to nonprofit organizations in board education, development, self-assessment, and leadership transitions. In addition to providing board development services to a variety of nonprofit organizations, she frequently serves as a speaker at leadership forums dedicated to governance and accountability. Nancy has served as a governing and advisory board member and board development consultant to numerous associations, foundations, charitable organizations, higher education institutions, and other nonprofit organizations. She is a member of the faculty of the Institute for Board Chairs and Presidents of Independent Colleges and Universities, sponsored by the Association of Governing Boards of Universities and Colleges, and ASAE & the Center for Association Leadership's Exceptional Boards program.

Nancy is the founding president of the National Center for Nonprofit Boards (now known as BoardSource), where she served as its first chief executive officer from 1987 to 1996. She is the author of *Culture of Inquiry: Healthy Debate in the Boardroom; Chief Executive Succession Planning: The Board's Role in Securing Your Organization's Future;* and *Advisory Councils.* She is a contributing author to *The Jossey-Bass Handbook of Nonprofit Leadership and Management,* and has written numerous articles and op-ed pieces. Nancy currently serves as a member of the Advisory Board of the Initiative on Social Enterprise at the Harvard Business School and the Review Panel of the NACD Director of the Year Award. She is a former chairman of the Board of Trustees of the Association Leadership Foundation of the Greater Washington Society of Association Executives. Nancy can be reached at www.nancyaxelrod.com.